Read for a Better World

KARATE
A First Look

KATIE PETERS

GRL Consultant, Diane Craig, Certified Literacy Specialist

Lerner Publications ◆ Minneapolis

Educator Toolbox

Reading books is a great way for kids to express what they're interested in. Before reading this title, ask the reader these questions:

> What do you think this book is about? Look at the cover for clues.
>
> What do you already know about karate?
>
> What do you want to learn about karate?

Let's Read Together

Encourage the reader to use the pictures to understand the text.

Point out when the reader successfully sounds out a word.

Praise the reader for recognizing sight words such as *it* and *is*.

TABLE OF CONTENTS

Karate 4

You Connect! 21

Social and Emotional Snapshot 22

Photo Glossary 23

Learn More 23

Index. .24

Karate

Karate is a sport.
Many kids do it.

We wear
white pants.
We wear a
white shirt.
They are loose.

Why are loose clothes good for this sport?

We wear belts.
We get new belts
as we get better.

We go to class.
The teacher has
a black belt.

We learn to punch.

We learn to block.

We learn to kick.
We use our
knees too.

Do you know
of other sports
like karate?

We practice
on a mat.
We don't hurt
each other.

Why should you do karate on a mat?

We get stronger.
But we learn it is best
not to fight.

Karate is fun!

You Connect!

Have you ever tried karate before?

What about karate seems most fun to you?

How could you get better at karate?

Social and Emotional Snapshot

Student voice is crucial to building reader confidence. Ask the reader:

> What is your favorite part of this book?

> What is something you learned from this book?

> Did this book remind you of any sports you play?

Opportunities for social and emotional learning are everywhere. How can you connect the topic of this book to the SEL competencies below?

> Responsible Decision-Making
> Self-Awareness
> Self-Management

Photo Glossary

belt

block

mat

teacher

Learn More

Downs, Kieran. *Karate*. Minneapolis: Bellwether Media, 2021.

Sterling, Holly. *Karate Kids*. Somerville, MA: Candlewick Press, 2020.

Vink, Amanda. *Karate*. New York: PowerKids Press, 2020.

Index

belts, 9, 10
block, 13

kick, 14
mat, 16, 17

practice, 16
punch, 12

Photo Acknowledgments

The images in this book are used with the permission of: © FatCamera/iStockphoto, pp. 4–5, 20; © JackF/iStockphoto, pp. 6–7; © Ancika/iStockphoto, pp. 8–9, 23 (belt, mat); © Gerville/iStockphoto, pp. 9, 12; © New Africa/Shutterstock Images, pp. 10–11, 14–15, 23 (teacher); © Lokibaho/iStockphoto, pp. 13, 23 (block); © kali9/iStockphoto, pp. 16–17; © 7stock/Shutterstock Images, pp. 16, 18–19.

Cover Photograph: © kali9/iStockphoto

Design Elements: © Mighty Media, Inc.

Lerner Publications Company
An imprint of Lerner Publishing Group, Inc.
241 First Avenue North
Minneapolis, MN 55401 USA

For reading levels and more information, look up this title at www.lernerbooks.com.

Main body text set in Mikado a Medium.
Typeface provided by Hannes von Doehren.

Library of Congress Cataloging-in-Publication Data

Names: Peters, Katie, author.
Title: Karate : a first look / Katie Peters.
Description: Minneapolis, MN : Lerner Publications, [2023] | Series: Read about sports. Read for a better world. | Includes bibliographical references and index. | Audience: Ages 5–8 | Audience: Grades K–1 | Summary: "Karate can make you stronger. Young learners will have fun learning what karate is and how to participate"– Provided by publisher.
Identifiers: LCCN 2022011585 (print) | LCCN 2022011586 (ebook) | ISBN 9781728475738 (library binding) | ISBN 9781728479064 (paperback) | ISBN 9781728484587 (ebook)
Subjects: LCSH: Karate—Juvenile literature.
Classification: LCC GV1114.3 .P48 2023 (print) | LCC GV1114.3 (ebook) | DDC 796.815/309–dc23

LC record available at https://lccn.loc.gov/2022011585
LC ebook record available at https://lccn.loc.gov/2022011586

Manufactured in the United States of America
1 - CG - 12/15/22